The Genesis Brides

By

SAM UEL T. CARSON

The Genesis Brides
Copyright © Samuel T. Carson 1992
First published 1992

ISBN   0   907927   79   3

AMBASSADOR PRODUCTIONS LTD
Providence House,
16 Hillview Avenue,
Belfast, BT5 6JR
U.K.

All Rights Reserved

Contents

Acknowledgements

The author acknowledges with gratitude all who helped and encouraged him in this project. Especially Warren Wiersbie who first read the manuscript. Thanks are also due to Isobel Jackson who spent many hours at her typewriter and to Susan and Samuel Bell who made many helpful suggestions.

DEDICATION

To Christine my wife, whose unfailing loyalty over all the years has meant so much to me

Foreword

This is the kind of book I wish had been available when I was in the pastorate and counselling couples preparing for marriage.

To begin with, this book is Biblical. After all, it is God Who established marriage; so we ought to get our guidance from Him. Everything written about marriage must be tested by the infallible Word of God lest we find ourselves building on the sand.

This book was written by an experienced and compassionate pastor who knows the Bible and the human heart. These brief chapters are filled with practical wisdom based on the Word of God.

This book is unique. I don't know that I have seen another like it. By introducing us to "Bible couples," Sam Carson both expounds and illustrates Biblical truths about marriage and the home. These studies are like a "fireside chat" with a beloved pastor who wants God's best for his people. He speaks the truth in love, and we are the better for it.

The message of this book is greatly needed today. I pray that it will have a wide ministry and great usefulness.

Warren W. Wiersbe
Author and Conference Speaker

Introduction

In recent years western society has experienced revolution in many areas of life, not least has this been so in the matter of marriage and divorce and remarriage after divorce. "The spirit abroad in the world to-day will be in the church to-morrow" is an old adage which has proved very true in regard to these things. It is not surprising that the intrusion of such issues into the life and counsels of the Christian Church has been followed by a plethora of books, dealing, from one standpoint or another, with the vexed questions thrown up by the new situations. As might be expected these books deal in the main with questions of divorce and re-marriage after divorce. That is not the purpose of this little volume. The intention is rather to focus the reader's mind on the uniqueness of the marriage bond itself. After all, prevention is better than a thousand cures and if this little book should help to develop a truer appreciation in the reader's mind of the integrity of the marriage bond then it will serve a useful purpose.

There are two ways in which the living God instructs His people through His word. One is by precept. Great principles are set forth in terms that are clear and plain. Line upon line, verse upon verse, precept upon precept. The other way is by displaying these same principles as they are worked out in the lives of His people. For instance, in the scriptures there is a clarion call to a life of faith. "Have faith

in God", "We walk by faith" etc. are watchwords of the
Christian life. So important is faith that we are told "without
faith it is impossible to please God." But what is faith? The
answer is given in the eleventh chapter of Hebrews. The
writer takes us on a journey through the Old Testament;
identifying for us here and there the worthies of faith. The
list is obviously not complete and yet when taken together
the varied facets of faith revealed in each character men-
tioned, give us a complete picture of what faith really is.
These histories of how divine grace wrought in such a great
variety of men and women - in a still greater variety of
circumstances and situations - are faithfully recorded as
patterns to guide us in our situations which are far more
similar to theirs than we sometimes imagine.

The book of Genesis calls attention to four women who
were united in marriage to four men, all of whom are
striking types of our Lord Jesus Christ. A brief outline of the
relationships that developed between these men and these
women is the theme of this book. It might be thought that
Sarah should have been included, making five in all. But she
was already the wife of Abraham before the God of glory
appeared to him and called him. For this reason Sarah is not
among the number dealt with here.

As recorded in scripture the story of the Genesis brides is
unsurpassed from a literary point of view. What joy and yet
what anguish, what depths of feeling and emotion lie hidden in these wonderful narratives. We learn here the uniqueness of the marriage bond; what kind of love it is that can
bind two human beings together in an abiding union.
Moreover Christians are here instructed in the amazing
ways of God's overruling providence, in which He causes
all things to work together for good to them that love Him.
And beyond all that we are here able to glimpse some of the
mysteries that enter into the heavenly union that exists
between Christ and His Church.

The pattern of this short volume then is to take these four
remarkable women married to four remarkable men and to
trace in those marriages things that foreshadow the union of

Christ and the Church; and to show how every marriage, and especially every Christian marriage, finds its true character set forth in that heavenly union. Apart from passing reference, the vexed questions of divorce and remarriage are not dealt with: the aim is rather to concentrate on the divine ideal for the marriage bond itself.

'And the Lord God said, It is not good that the man should be alone: I will make him an help meet for him.

And out of the ground the Lord God formed every beast of the field, and every fowl of the air; and brought them unto Adam to see what he would call them: and whatsoever Adam called every living creature, that was the name thereof.

And Adam gave names to all cattle, and to the fowl of the air, and to every beast of the field; but for Adam there was not found a help meet for him.

And the Lord God caused a deep sleep to fall upon Adam, and he slept: and he took one of his ribs, and closed up the flesh instead thereof:

And Adam said, This is now bone of my bones, and flesh of my flesh: she shall be called Woman, because she was taken out of Man.

Therefore shall a man leave his father and his mother, and shall cleave unto his wife and they shall be one flesh.'

~ From Genesis Chapter Two

Adam's Bride

"He who made them in the beginning made them male and female and said, For this cause shall a man leave father and mother, and shall cleave to his wife; and they twain shall be one flesh." Matthew 19:4, 5.

Next to destinies, the human preoccupation across the generations has been with origins. How did it all begin? Where did it all come from? Where have we ourselves come from? The book of Genesis is the book of beginnings. Here we have the origin of the created order and of the human race itself. Here we have the first man, Adam, and the first woman, Eve. While still only in the second chapter of Genesis we are confronted with the first marriage, the prototype of every true marriage, and a foreshadowing of the heavenly union between Christ and His Church.

Genesis has aptly been called the seed plot of the whole Bible. All the great themes of Holy Scripture are found here in germ form. This probably explains why it has been singled out for attack more than any other of the sixty-six books. But Genesis has been wonderfully preserved and in spite of repeated and sustained onslaught it has stood across the centuries and abides unscathed to this day. We can have no difficulty in accepting the authority of Genesis, since the Lord Jesus Christ, the Son of God, acknowledged it to be the very word of God. How daring for unbelieving men to reject as spurious the very writings which our divine Saviour has established as being of supreme authority. (See Luke 24: 27) All who bow to the Lordship of Christ must reverently and sincerely recognise the Divine inspiration of the Genesis record.

The first chapter of Genesis takes us in order through the six workdays of God which, together with the Sabbath of rest, are commonly called creation week. On the sixth day God said, "Let us make man in our image, after our likeness." (Gen. 1: 26) The crowning act of creation was the creation of man: "God created man in His own image, in the image of God made He him." (Gen. 1: 27) It has been said that such is the pride of the human heart, had God created man first he would have claimed the rest of the work as his own. But man was created last. He was then exalted to the apex of the whole created order and all things were placed in submission beneath his feet. It is here that the Genesis record stands opposed to the evolutionary theories developed over the last one hundred years but now largely discredited. Evolution postulates man on the bottom rung of the ladder, struggling to climb to the top. Hence the oft quoted phrase, "the ascent of man". But the Bible teaches the descent of man. He began at the top and then fell, through his sin and disobedience.

That the existence of man is not an accident of evolution but the creative act of the living God, was confirmed by Jesus. When questioned on the subject of divorce, He carried His hearers back beyond Moses and the law to the first chapter of Genesis and declared, "He who made them in the beginning...." (Matt. 19: 4) It follows as a matter of course therefore, that the Creator has certain creatorial rights of which the creature must ever be mindful. In one of the wisdom books of scripture Solomon said, "Rejoice O young man in your youth and let your heart cheer you in the days of your youth, and walk in the ways of your heart and in the sight of your eyes; but know this, that for all these things God will bring you into judgment." (Eccl. 11: 9) Ultimately we are all accountable to God: none of us can escape the judgment of God. (Rom. 14: 12)

In considering the marriage bond we must always bear in mind that marriage is first and foremost a creation ordinance. It was ordained for the benefit and well-being of the human family as a whole, and it must therefore be governed by those principles upon which it was instituted in the beginning by the Creator Himself. The civil law may alter to take account of the ebb and flow of public opinion, but God does not change and we must bow to those great principles which He has given us if family life, and ultimately society itself, are to be preserved from self-destruction.

THE CREATION OF ADAM

The work of the sixth day was actually in two parts. God created the man and after that the woman and thus male and female created He them. Of the first part of that day's work we read "the Lord God formed man of the dust of the ground and breathed into his nostrils the breath of life and man became a living soul." (Gen. 2: 7) That the man was created first and then the woman was not without significance, for the order is not only stated, but at the end of the chapter it is emphasised. Moreover, Paul highlights God's order in creation to demonstrate the truth of headship; and to regulate the subsequent relationship of husband and wife in the family, and of men and women in the assembly.

When the man, as distinct from the woman, had been formed, God said, "it is not good that the man should be alone; I will make him a help meet for him." (Gen. 2: 18) This statement does not mean that there is anything inherently wrong in the unmarried state but that God's ideal from the beginning has been a partnership. The word translated "helpmeet" might better be rendered "counterpart". God's ideal has always been a partnership, between a man and a woman, the one being the precise counterpart of the other. The fact that God created the woman to be the specific counterpart of the man rules out such marriages as between man and man, or woman and woman, for such are not true marriages at all. The only marriage permitted by God is between a man and a woman who have been lawfully joined together.

In this connection it should also be noted that at the end of the Old Testament the prophet Malachi asked a most arresting question: why did God make just one woman for Adam? After all, He had the residue of the Spirit, He could have made two or several but He made just one. (Mal. 2: 15)The question is rhetorical and the prophet supplies the answer. The Creator's plain intention from the beginning was that each man would be a 'one woman' man. But the prophet also gave a further reason by pointing to God's concern for the well-being of the offspring of the marriage. A matter, it must be said, that is causing considerable alarm to all responsible and informed members of contemporary society. He would be naive indeed, who considered the frightening statistics on child abuse wholly unrelated to the many and complex issues raised by society's current attitude to the marriage bond.

The reference to a helpmeet or a counterpart is also a clear and concise statement on the equality of the sexes. He who made them in the beginning, while He made them fearfully and wonderfully different, made them intrinsically equal. The woman is the exact counterpart of the man physically, intellectually and in every other way. We must be careful not to attempt to make them more equal than God has made them. Each of us has two hands. They are both equal and yet they are different. One is a right hand, the other a left. Leave them as God made them and they can work in complete and perfect harmony. How clumsy we should become if, in trying to make them more equal we reversed the fingers and thumb of one hand so as to make them both right or both left hands.

Again it has often been pointed out that God did not take a bone from Adam's head, for the woman was not intended to be his superior, nor from his foot for then she might have been considered his inferior; he took a bone from his side teaching us that the woman is the equal of the man, his companion and true helpmeet. Within the framework of a happy marriage the woman is not a second class partner nor will she regard herself as such. On the contrary, she and her husband will both rejoice in the words of Peter when he wrote of them being "heirs together of the grace of life." (1st Pet. 3: 7)

THE GREATNESS OF THE FIRST MAN

Now before the creation of the woman is described, we have an event which expresses the greatness of the man and by implication the greatness of the woman as well, since she is the exact counterpart of the man.

The whole creation was caused to pass before Adam that he might name each individual part of it, and whatever he called it, that was the name by which it became known and is still known to this day. The organisational details of the naming ceremony are withheld from us, but we do know that each separate species of the animal kingdom was identified by name. The task of evaluating the different kinds of animals and the privilege of putting a name upon each of them was given to Adam, the original man.

Laying aside, for the moment, what we know of the man Christ Jesus, we have really no conception of how great that man was who came directly from the hand of God. He was a man of amazing insight and of giant intellect. The best specimen of humanity known to us is only a pale reflection of that original man. In addition, a telling phrase is used at this point: "for Adam there was not found a help meet for him." (Gen. 2: 20) A fit companion for the man could not be supplied from the lower creation; a further act of creation was required. Surely this bears witness to the superiority of the human over the animal creation. The gulf between the two has been and remains unbridgeable.

Adam could name the animals and rule them, but he could not relate to them on an equal plane for he belonged to a different order of creation. He alone was made in the image of God. Eve, on the other hand, while distinct from

Adam was part of him, his complement, his fulness. He could delight in her and together they could enjoy the provisions of the world around them and above all the privilege of communion with the God of their creation.

ADAM'S BRIDE

The details of the woman's creation are most interesting. (Gen. 2: 22) Three things took place. Having first caused Adam to go down into a deep sleep, God took a rib from his side. We may call this the first anesthetic and the first surgical operation. Certainly the spiritual mind can see in it the death of our Lord Jesus Christ, for both in Adam's deep sleep and in Jesus' death, God did something that had to be done, something that only God could do and something that will never need to be done again. "It is finished" was the Crucified's all important cry from the cross. Everything that required to be done for our salvation was done when Jesus bled and died. We rest secure in the completeness of the sacrifice that was made by the offering of the body of Jesus Christ once and for all.

In the second place, from that rib God built a woman, for "built" is the force of the word "made" in the text. (Gen 2: 22)Indeed this is the precise rendering of it in the New King James Version. This plainly illustrates God's activity in this present age. In response to Simon Peter's confession at Caesarea Philippi, Jesus said, "I will build my Church, and the gates of hell shall not prevail against it," (Matt. 16: 18)and so throughout his age God has been engaged in the mighty enterprise of building the Church. The divinely appointed way of accomplishing this is through the preaching of the gospel. "Announce the glad tidings to every creature" (Mark 16: 15) was the commission the risen Christ gave to His own, and the gospel of Christ is said to be the power (dynamite) of God unto salvation to every one who believes. (Rom. 1: 16) Each new believer is a member of this body, a stone in this building which all the while is growing unto an holy temple in the Lord. (Eph. 2: 21) The pledge to build the Church, given at Caesarea, still holds good, and the work continues to this day.

Then, thirdly, God took the woman and brought her and presented her to Adam to be his bride. This quite clearly anticipates a day that is still to be, when the church will be presented to Christ, a glorious Church, a spotless bride. (Rev. 19: 7, 8)

THE MARRIAGE BOND

From all this it should not be difficult to see how Adam and Eve typify Christ and His Church. When we apprehend that, we can understand what the marriage bond really is according to God's ideal. It is a tie formed between a man and a woman after the pattern of that mystical union which exists between Christ and His Church. It is an earthly bond that takes its character from the heavenly union.

The nature of this union is so wonderful that Adam could say of Eve, "this is now bone of my bone and flesh of my flesh." . (Gen. 2: 23) Separating bone from bone, and flesh from flesh, is always a very serious matter. Hence we must be exceedingly careful in judging matters of a matrimonial nature, lest we contribute to a diminishing of the significance of the marriage bond. We can yield too quickly to the spirit of easy compromise so prevalent in today's society. Untold damage is done when we accommodate biblical principles to the changing moods of a godless world. Nor must we ever forget that between Christ and His Church there is an abiding union, a tie which shall never be broken. The marriage bond according to the divine ideal is a life long union of a man and a woman who have been lawfully joined together.

THE PRINCIPLE OF HEADSHIP

Ere the record concludes the priority of the man is once again stressed. The counterpart of Adam was called woman because she was taken out of the man. Paul put it like this: "Adam was first formed, then Eve." . (1st Tim. 2: 13) Moreover it is an essential feature of the marriage bond that the man shall leave his father and his mother and shall cleave unto his wife and they shall be one flesh. (Gen. 2: 24) We should note the order in which these things are stated. Becoming one flesh is the physical side of marriage. It must be understood, however, that while all truly married couples have become one flesh not all who have become one flesh are truly married. Paul insisted that he that is joined to a harlot is one flesh, but such a union cannot be considered a marriage in any meaningful sense.

Since all sexual intercourse issues in the parties concerned becoming one flesh, it follows that for a married person to engage in such activity outside the marriage bond is to destroy the unique "one flesh" relationship. Of course "one flesh" denotes more than the physical aspect of marriage. It means that two distinct and separate personalities have come together in such a way that they are now no longer two but one. Paul said "He that loves his wife loves himself and no man ever hated his own flesh." (Eph. 5: 28, 29) Marriage is more than just a union: it is a oneness.

For a man and a woman simply to agree to live together as husband and wife does not constitute a marriage. The presence of a formal and legally binding contract that commits the parties to each other is essential if the union is to be recognised as marriage. In scriptural terms there must be a leaving and a cleaving and it is noteworthy that these come first. These two words are correlatives, the latter necessitates the former. There cannot be a true cleaving without a corresponding leaving. That there are these two sides to marriage must not be ignored.

LEAVING. "For this cause shall a man leave his father and mother....." (Eph. 5: 31) That is, since God made woman for him, the man must leave his parents in order to establish his own family. By the same token the marriage ceremony reaches a point where the question is asked, "Who giveth this woman to be married to this man?" The reply that is made, usually by the bride's father is, "I do." Thus the bride is formally given away to become part of a wholly new relationship.

The leaving is sometimes painful for the parents, especially if there are factors in the marriage which, as they see them, gives cause for concern, or if the newly weds are not only leaving the family home but are, for instance, going abroad to live. Nevertheless, wise parents will recognise the new situation, and while being always available to help and counsel will be careful not to interfere on one side or the other, for such interference usually puts strains upon the fledgling marriage and sometimes can occasion its failure.

The leaving can be difficult for the newly married couple also. Hitherto they have been able to fall back upon their parents, but now they must meet problems as they arise and solve them in their own way. They may seek advice from their parents, and others, but they must recognise their new status and together build up their own relationship.

CLEAVING. The other side of the coin is the cleaving. "A man shall leave his father and mother and shall cleave unto his wife." (Eph. 5: 31) We are told that the Hebrew word translated "cleave" literally means "to be glued together." In marriage the man and his wife are intended to stick together. That is why adultery is so grievous. It is a third party coming between a man and a woman already glued together in God's sight. The cleaving teaches quite plainly that God instituted marriage on a monogamous basis. It is true that in certain very exceptional cases we read of polygamy in the Old Testament yet the fact is, that such marriages were at variance with marriage as established by God and the record of them nearly always proves that such practice, far from bringing happiness, brought untold sorrow in its train. The leaving and the cleaving do not mean an abandoning of parents on the one hand, or offspring on the other, but rather the recognition that a new family unit has been formed and a new headship established.

Within the marriage bond, therefore, God has established a certain order and within that order He has vested headship in the man. Before marriage the partners were subject to the headship of their respective parents but now a wholly new headship has been created. Paul therefore exhorts "wives submit yourselves to your own husbands and husbands love your wives." (Eph. 5: 22) There is nothing tyrannical or legalistic about this. On the contrary, the apostle asserts the loving character of the relationship. The submission of the one is of the same nature as the Church's subjection to Christ while the love of the other derives its inspiration from Christ's love, "who loved the Church and gave Himself for it." (Eph. 5: 25)

When headship is discussed it is usually the subjective side that is talked about; the other, equally important, authority side is often overlooked. If the headship has been vested in the man then he ought to be exercising leadership in both family and assembly life. That there is great weakness in both areas is becoming increasingly apparent. The failure is perhaps more immediately recognisable in the Church. Take, for instance, the field of missionary endeavour; the preponderance of women on the mission field is reaching such proportions that it is almost a reproach to the Christian Church. Every mission administrator is grateful for the devotion of that noble band of godly women who have gone forth to carry the gospel of Christ to others, but where are their male counterparts? The same weakness can be seen at the local level. Some churches still adhere to the principle of the silence or comparative silence of women in the public gatherings. The correlative of this is that exercised brothers should give a definite lead in prayer and worship. In fact the life of many churches is being stifled by a situation that has arisen, where the sisters can't and the brethren won't. Headship places upon the head a responsibility that must not be disregarded.

Rise up, O men of God
Have done with lesser things
Give heart and soul and mind and strength
To serve the King of Kings

WHEN PROBLEMS ARISE

In the nature of things no matter how well the domestic circle may be ordered, issues will from time to time arise and problems will present themselves. Many of these matters will admit a fairly straightforward solution but others will prove more difficult. A believing husband and wife will talk all these things over and pray about them. Normally this will result in both being of one mind in their response. If however this should not be so, headship means that normally the onus is upon the husband to take responsibility for the ultimate decision, and the onus is upon the wife to go along with, and support her husband in his decision. The outworking of this will in turn present to the children in the home an object lesson on what submission actually is, and will enable them to see the vital principle of true obedience objectively set forth, in the relationship of their parents to each other and to the Lord.

The same principle is to mark the assembly. The woman by recognising her subjection to the man and the man his subjection to Christ will enable both the woman and the man, each acknowledging God's order, to walk together in subjection to the ultimate headship of Christ. (1st Cor. 11: 3) In turn such godly order will make the assembly an object lesson (Eph 2: 7, 3: 10) to men and to angels showing them something of the manifold wisdom of God and the exceeding riches of the divine grace that can take rebel sinners, subdue their rebellious hearts and bring them into such a place of subjection where they give full and glad obedience to the God of their salvation. Nor does this affect the matter of equality. It is rather order and priority that are in view. Nowhere is this more clearly seen than in the case of the Son of God Himself, Who, while co-equal with the Father, lived upon this earth in subjection to the Father. Characteristically He said on one occasion, "my meat is to do the will of Him that sent me" (John 4: 34) and in this, as in all else, He left us an example that we should follow.

CHRIST AND THE CHURCH

But the parallels between Adam and Eve on the one hand and Christ and the Church on the other do not stop there. When God created the man He formed him of the dust of the ground, and breathed into him the breath of life, and the man became a living soul; but when He created the woman there was no further breathing of God. Eve's existence derived from Adam. Although distinct from him, she was a part of him. In a word, his life was her life. As has already been noted the first marriage was more than a union, it was a oneness. Writing to the Church at Corinth Paul used the analogy of the human body: "as the body is one, and has many members, and all the members of that one body, being many, are one body, so also is Christ." (1st Cor. 12: 12) (The context makes it clear that the reference is not to Christ personal but to Christ mystical, i.e. Christ and the Church.) Here is the antitype of Eve's relationship to Adam. The Church has no existence apart from Christ. His life is her life. "Your life is hid with Christ in God," wrote Paul; and again "when Christ who is our life shall appear then shall we also appear with Him in glory." (Col. 3: 3, 4)

In the same way within the marriage bond the wife's life is bound up with that of her husband. It was so in the first marriage. "God created man (singular) in His own image, in the image of God created He them (Plural). And God blessed them and said "....have dominion....over every living thing...." (Gen. 1: 28) It is inconceivable that Eve pursued a path that was independent of Adam. The clear inference is that just as in the first instance the Church is subject to Christ and again that every member of the human body takes its direction from the head, so the wife shall look to her husband and recognise the headship that is vested in him by God. If a woman feels she is not able or willing to do this she should not marry. The rule for every woman is, do not marry a man you are not able to look up to and respect.

The fact that Adam and Eve failed and by their failure occasioned the fall only serves to emphasise the abiding character of divine principles. The living God has now taken up His purpose for the earth in a second man, a last Adam, the Lord from heaven. In a coming day all things both in heaven and on earth will be harmonised and headed up in Him and in that day when He shall reign, the Church shall reign with Him.(Eph. 1: 10)This means that the ultimate pattern for the marriage bond is not Adam and Eve but, as has been shown, Christ and the Church.

• • •

"*And Abraham was old, and well stricken in age: and the Lord had blessed Abraham in all things.*

And Abraham said unto his eldest servant of his house, that ruled over all that he had, Put, I pray thee, thy hand under my thigh:

And I will make thee swear by the Lord, the God of heaven, and the God of the earth, that thou shalt not take a wife unto my son of the daughters of the Canaanites, among whom I dwell:

But thou shalt go unto my country, and to my kindred, and take a wife unto my son Isaac.

And the servant said unto him, suppose the woman will not be willing to follow me unto this land: must I needs bring thy son again unto the land from whence thou camest?

And Abraham said unto him, Beware thou that thou bring not my son thither again.

The Lord God of heaven, which took me from my Father's house, and from the land of my kindred, and which spake unto me, and that swear unto me saying, Unto thy seed will I give this land; he shall send his angel before thee, and thou shalt take a wife unto my son from thence.

And if the woman will not be willing to follow thee, then thou shalt be clear from this my oath: only bring not my son thither again.

And the servant put his hand under the thigh of Abraham his master, and swear to him concerning that matter.

And Rebekah arose, and her damsels, and they rode upon the camels, and followed the man: and the servant took Rebekah and went his way.

And Isaac came from the way of the well Lahai-roi; for he dwelt in the south country.

And Rebekah lifted up her eyes, and when she saw Isaac, she alighted from off the camel.

For she had said unto the servant, What man is this that walketh in the field to meet us? And the servant had said, It is my master: therefore she took a vail, and covered herself.

And the servant told Isaac all things that he had done.

And Isaac brought her into his mother Sarah's tent, and took Rebekah, and she became his wife; and he loved her: and Isaac was comforted after his mother's death."

~ From Genesis Chapter Twenty Four

Isaac's Bride

"Whoso findeth a wife findeth a good thing and obtains favour of the Lord." Proverbs 18: 22.

Having considered how God established human society upon the earth and how He instituted the marriage bond, we now move on to the vitally important matter of choosing a life partner. Many years of counselling couples, both before and after marriage, has confirmed just how unrealistic it is to approach such a matter with a legal code or a set of rules in one's hand. But in this as in every other area of life, God has not left us to our own devices. He has given us His word and here the sacred scriptures are not found wanting.

In the record of Abraham sending his nameless servant to Mesopotamia to seek a bride for Isaac we are given a remarkably detailed and comprehensive outline of those guiding principles which should serve to guide the Christian who is contemplating marriage. The first and obvious detail that catches our attention is that one of the longest chapters in the whole Bible is given over in its entirety to the matter of finding Isaac's bride. And what a chapter it is. Alexander Whyte said of this ancient record - "a sweeter chapter was never written than the twenty-fourth of Genesis...The picture of the aged Abraham swearing his most trusty servant about a bride for his son Isaac; the servant's journey to Padan-aram in the Far East; Rebekah, first at the well, and then in her mother's house; and then her first sight of her future husband - that long chapter is a perfect gem of ancient authorship." This in itself should alert us to the importance attached to the matter in hand.

The chapter before us is certainly pertinent to our subject, and that for a number of reasons. It gives us an overview of God's gracious purposes for His people in this age. We also see reflected in it and especially in Rebekah how God deals with us as individual believers, and besides this we find here some practical implications of special relevance to those stepping out upon married life; these we see in the conduct of Abraham's servant.

The living God had wondrous purposes in His heart for the chosen nation which sprang from Abraham. Next in line to Abraham was Isaac and through him the purpose of God would flow and the chosen race would develop. (Gen. 17: 19) It was necessary therefore, that the one chosen to be Isaac's wife should be someone who would be in sympathy with God's will for Him. It is a tenet of Christian belief that God has a plan and purpose for the lives of His people.

Before even He formed us, He mapped out a path for us. Moreover there is a niche in God's overall programme for each of us to fill. Does it need to be argued then that someone out of sympathy with such thoughts would be wholly unsuitable as a life partner for one who is seeking to walk with God?

AN OVERVIEW OF GOD'S PURPOSE

The story begins in the Father's house where three persons only are in view, the father (Abraham), the son (Isaac) and the nameless servant. By this we are reminded of the Father's house on high and of the fact that the God of scripture is a triune God. (Matt. 28: 19) There are three persons in the Godhead, the Father, the Son and the Holy Spirit, the same in substance, and equal in power and glory. The doctrine of the Trinity is of crucial importance; it lies at the heart of the Christian faith and is basic to a true understanding of our Saviour's death upon the Cross.

The Cross is something more tham simply an angry God punishing an innocent *victim*, a disinterested third party, in order that the guilty might go free. This is a travesty of truth for in such a scenario there is neither justice nor mercy. We must see the Cross in the light of the Trinity. Since God, in the mystery of His being, is three persons yet one God, He is able at one and the same time, to both inflict and bear punishment. This He did at Calvary. There God judged our sins while at the same time He bore that judgment in the person of His Son, our Lord Jesus Christ. And now we estranged sinners can be reconciled to God through the death of His Son. (Rom. 5: 10)

RELATIONSHIPS

But the doctrine of the Trinity also raises for us the matter of relationships within the Godhead. We learn a lot about human relationships by studying those within the Godhead. Take the most precious of human relationships. Parents learn best how to relate to their children and vice versa by studying how the Father related to the Son and the Son to the Father during the thirty-three years of the Son's pilgrimage here upon earth. In the same way husbands and wives learn best how to relate to each other by pondering the union that exists between Christ and the Church.

In Abraham's home we can discern outlines of those heavenly relationships from which our own, in our various domestic circles, should take their character. In Abraham's plans for Isaac we are given a wonderful insight into the purpose of our heavenly Father for His Son. Isaac was last seen at Mount Moriah where he was laid upon the altar of sacrifice. (Gen. 22: 9) Then he was taken up from the altar, in figure raised from the dead, and now we find him back again in the father's house. Instinctively Abraham's mind turned to the vital matter of finding a bride for Isaac; who undoubtedly speaks to us of our Lord Jesus Christ.

Somewhere in the dateless past an everlasting covenant was made between the persons of the Godhead. The Father covenanted to give a bride to His Son. In the fulness of time the Son came forth. He lived and died, and on the third day, He rose from the dead. In resurrection He is said to have been "brought again from the dead by the blood of the everlasting covenant."(Hebs. 13: 20)He has now returned to heaven itself from whence He will come again according to His promise. In the meantime the Father has sent the Holy Spirit into the world to take out of it a bride for His Son; that bride is the Church. When the work is complete Christ will come and the Church will be presented to Him a glorious Church having neither spot nor wrinkle nor any such thing. (Eph. 5: 27)

THE MISSION OF THE SPIRIT

The timing of the sending forth of Abraham's servant should not be overlooked. Isaac had passed through death (albeit in figure) and he was now back again in the father's house before the servant was launched upon his ministry. By the same token the third person of the Trinity did not come forth while the second person was still upon the earth. We read in John's Gospel that the Holy Spirit was not yet given because Jesus was not yet glorified. (John 7: 39)The coming into the world of the Holy Spirit, of whom the nameless servant is a type, had to await the return of Jesus to heaven.

Of course the Holy Spirit has been at work in the world from the beginning but it would appear that throughout the Old Testament period, as in the case of Samson, He came upon certain persons at certain times and for certain specific purposes. (Jud. 14: 6, 19) When he came at Pentecost however, the Holy Spirit came to take up residence upon the earth. His dwelling was to be the Church, (Eph. 2: 22) brought into being by His coming and still in the course of preparation.

Uniquely He indwells the Church by indwelling each individual member of it. The Lord Jesus anticipated this in the upper room. Having announced to His disciples His own departure to the Father, He then gave them this pledge, "I will pray the Father and He will send you another comforter even the Spirit of truth...." Thus the Saviour revealed to His own the coming of the Holy Spirit to indwell God's people.

The primary mission of the Holy Spirit in the world today, is not so much to do something in the world but to take something out of it. His purpose is not world improvement but to call out from among all peoples, a people for the Saviour's Name. (Acts 15: 14) He accomplishes this purpose through the preaching of the gospel and those thus called out form the Church, which is to be presented to Christ by and by as His bride. Abraham's servant did not go to Mesopotamia to get involved in the affairs of that place. He kept expressly to his task. Indeed, that he pursued his goal with such singleness of purpose and such a sense of urgency, is in itself a rebuke to us in our worldly-wise ways. As Christians we tend to become involved in so much that is not our business while we neglect our supreme task of preaching the gospel to every creature.

GOD'S WAY WITH US

(i) How it Begins
How the work was done and the commission fulfilled is best told by Rebekah herself. In the first instance she must relate how it all began. One day as she was going about her normal business she met a man who told her things she had never heard before; he showed her things that she had never seen before. All these things found their centre in a certain man called Isaac. Her interest was arrested, and her heart was stirred for the nameless servant did his work well. He pressed his advantage until Rebekah was brought to a place where a decision had to be made.

The issue was simple and the matter urgent: the question demanding her decision was this: "wilt thou go with this man?" It was with quiet conviction and calm assurance she responded, saying quite simply, "I will go." All who are the Lord's are able to read, to varying degrees, the story of their own conversion in the experience of Rebekah. The Holy Spirit began dealing with us, He arrested us and brought us individually to face up to the all-important question, "What shall I do then with Jesus which is called Christ?" (Matt. 27: 22) Our response was similar to that of Rebekah: we were brought in repentance and faith to say, "I will", to Christ.

> *Jesus I will trust thee*
> *Trust thee with my soul*
> *Guilty, lost and helpless*
> *Thou canst make me whole.*

Only the Holy Spirit can bring sinners to that place of faith in Christ. Well intentioned Christians sometimes bring inordinate pressure to bear upon individuals, and especially upon those who are young, to make a decision for which they are not prepared by the Holy Spirit; this is probably to do irreparable harm.

Having said that, it is very important to see that while we are saved through individual faith in Christ; none of us is saved in isolation. All who in this age trust in the Saviour's Name are at that same moment joined to the Lord as members of His body. They become "in Christ." They are incorporated into that mystical body and become part of that Church which is to be Christ's bride. They not only share in the value of the atoning sacrifice of Christ, they are also made partakers of the Holy Spirit's baptism, which took place at Pentecost, and thus they are constituted one body in Christ. (1st Cor. 12: 13)

(ii) How it Continues

But Rebekah must go further and tell how the story continued. As the caravan moved off in the direction of Abraham's house, a long journey lay ahead. Rebekah would have to pass through a waste howling wilderness and cross a trackless desert. Left to herself and her own resources she could not have made it. Happily the nameless servant who had begun a good work in her did not abandon her. He went before and all the   long journey through she simply "followed the man."

Rebekah did not know the way but she followed one who did. Similarly it is ours who have trusted the Saviour to be "led by the Spirit". Our faith in Christ is not the end of the matter; it rather marks the beginning of a journey which bears us through this barren land, this vale of tears and up to the Father's house. Confiding in our own strength we only stumble and fall but in the person of the indwelling Holy Spirit, God has given us an unfailing guide who leads us with unerring step. He leads according to the word of truth and never contrary to that word. (Psa. 119: 105)

The Christian life is a life of faith. Each step is taken in dependence upon Him whose word is a lamp to our feet and a light to our path. Should we be in doubt about His leading in any given circumstance, we turn to that word and the mists are dispelled and our path becomes clear. He does not show us the end of the road but He assures us that when we obey Him in taking one step, He will give us light to take another. Moreover besides pointing the way He promises to go with us by His Spirit for He has said, "My presence shall go with you and I will never leave you nor forsake you." (Hebs. 13: 5)

(iii) How it Will End

The story however is not yet complete. Rebekah must tell how it all ended. A point was reached when she saw one coning to meet her. "Who is this?" she enquired of the nameless servant, who whispered softly in her ear, "it is my Master" and for the first time she saw Isaac. Often with the eyes of her heart she had pictured him but that was only the vision of faith. Now faith gave place to sight and she found herself face to face with Isaac. How often she had heard of him, how much she had been told about him, but now she could see him as he is. She saw him for whom she had forsaken all: her father's house and all that Mesopotamia held for her. Our position is akin to that of Rebekah. We love one whom we have never seen. That is something this foolish world cannot quite understand. The apostle Peter expressed it like this: "Whom having not seen, you love; in whom, though now you see Him not, yet believing, you rejoice with joy unspeakable and full of glory." (1st Pet. 1: 8) Our blessed hope is that Christ will come and we shall be caught up to meet Him, to see Him, to be like Him and to be with Him.

> *Face to face with Christ my Saviour,*
> *Face to face what will it be;*
> *When with rapture I behold Him*
> *Jesus Christ who died for me.*

Christ Himself shall greet us. He shall say, "my oxen and my fatlings are killed, come for all things are now ready." He shall conduct us to his banqueting house where we shall sit under His shadow, and His banner over us will be love. Then shall take place the marriage of the Lamb when the whole church arrayed in fine linen, clean and white shall be presented in the glory of His presence with exceeding great joy. (Rev. 19: 7)

As the time of the meeting drew near Rebekah did something that was very simple, yet full of significance. She took a veil and covered herself. She would not be found unprepared for the meeting with Isaac. We too want to be ready for the meeting with the heavenly Isaac. If we are not saved we are not ready. And yet there is more to being ready than being saved. Being ready involves fidelity to His Name in a world in which He is still despised and rejected. It involves faithfulness in His service as He said to His disciples: "blessed is that servant, whom his lord when he comes shall find so doing." (Luke 12: 43) We must gird ourselves and so bear ourselves that in that day we shall not be ashamed before Him.

In a previous chapter attention was called to the fact that the marriage relationship requires a leaving and a cleaving. Rebekah sets forth the leaving side of things. She had left her father's house, her home and her country, all for the love of

Isaac. To take a place of subjection to the one she loved was the most natural thing for her to do. Perhaps this is the real meaning of the veil; certainly the head covering elsewhere in scripture signifies the principle of subjection. (1st Cor. 11: 5) This much is clear: she covered herself. That is the secret of being ready to meet the Saviour. We must be able to say even now "not I but Christ." Self must be hidden for no flesh shall glory in His presence. Rebekah was ready at last to meet Isaac. All the desert was past, the vale of tears had been crossed -

> *Behind her all of sorrow*
> *And nought but joy before.*

PRACTICAL IMPLICATIONS

Serious and searching practical issues arise from all that we have been considering. Is any one today seeking a marriage partner? Such a person should study carefully the conduct of Abraham's servant for he exhibits great principles of guidance in matters of this nature.

In the course of a normal lifetime, and laying aside those decisions that are made for us in childhood, the decisions of far reaching consequence we are called to make must be legion. None is more important than our response to the gospel and our attitude to Christ for that is of eternal significance. After that, however, the most important issue must surely be the choice of a life partner if such should be sought. It may be that some settle this question on the basis of cold calculation, but they must be few. For the vast majority, the decision is charged with very deep emotion. That "there's nothing as bad as a bad marriage" may be an old saying, but its truth has been demonstrated a thousandfold in every generation. Conversely, a happy marriage partnership is a jewel of priceless worth.

UNEQUAL YOKE

For a believer to marry an unbeliever would constitute an unequal yoke and would be a clear violation of what God has enjoined upon His people. (2nd Cor. 6: 14) This is a principle that needs to be stressed in a day when the frontiers of light and darkness have become somewhat blurred. The mighty David, the sweet psalmist of Israel, the man after God's own heart failed just here, and reaped a terrible harvest. He married a pagan woman called Maacha who came from Geshur. (2nd Sam. 3: 3) She became the mother of Absalom who wrought mischief for David both in his family and in the wider circle of the kingdom.

Another of David's line was Jehoshaphat who in many ways was a good king over the house of Judah. His son Jehoram took to wife Athaliah the daughter of the wicked Ahab and Jezebel. (2nd Chron. 22: 11) She exercised a profound and baneful influence over both her husband and his successor, an influence that extended even to the third generation. Alas, it would appear that Jehoram's father had encouraged the marriage, doubtless for political reasons, thinking perhaps that the marriage would somehow bring the divided kingdom together again. Instead it came within a whisper of wiping out David's royal line. Only the faithfulness of God to the covenant He had made with His servant David saved the life of Joash and preserved the royal house from extinction.

ONLY IN THE LORD

And so by example as well as by precept the most solemn warnings are given in scripture against unequal yoke in marriage as well as in other areas of life. At the same time it must be obvious that the mere fact that both partners are "in Christ" is not of itself a sufficient ground for marriage. "Only in the Lord" is the Pauline expression used when the subject of Christian marriage is under discussion. (1st Cor. 7: 39) This surely means that as a prerequisite to a truly

Christian marriage there will be, on the part of the man and the woman, a waiting upon God in subjection to the Lordship of Christ, and a definite seeking after the leading of the Holy Spirit.

The servant of Abraham teaches us a great deal in this respect. His greatest priority was not to find a bride but rather to walk in the pathway of God's will. It is as we set ourselves to stand perfect and complete in all the will of God that we shall know God's gracious provision for us. The first thing Abraham's servant did was to wait upon God in prayer and to seek some divine seal upon the matter in hand. Nor was he disappointed for he was able to worship God who made his journey prosperous and in the end he could say, "I being in the way, the Lord led me." (Gen. 24: 27)

The selection of a bride for Isaac was a matter of very far reaching consequence. By the same token the choosing of a life partner is the most important decision, after conversion, that the Christian is called upon to make. It must not be made lightly but seriously, reverently, with true affection and in dependence upon God. These features are strikingly exemplified in the application of Abraham's servant to his task.

MEANINGFUL SIGNS

A matter that is forced upon our attention as we consider the movements of Abraham's servant is how the circumstances flowed together to confirm in his mind the rightness of his path. Nothing had to be twisted or forced into place. He was encouraged by the readiness of Rebekah to water the camels and then by the disclosure of Rebekah's background. On top of this there was the hospitality extended to him not only by Rebekah but also by her people. Even then he still waited upon God: "the man wondering held his peace." (Gen. 24: 21)

It is impossible simultaneously to wait upon God and act in haste. A moment would arrive when things must be brought to a decision but in the meanwhile time must be allowed for the God who "works all things after the counsel of His own will" (Eph. 1: 11) to bring to maturity those circumstances that would issue in Isaac and Rebekah being together in a permanent happy union. That marriage which is the result of engineering on the part of one partner or both or perhaps some third party is unlikely to be a happy one. The rule must always be to make haste slowly when the aim is something of a permanent nature. Marriage is ideally a lifelong union and it invariably proves to be this for those whom God has joined together.

The abiding appeal of the ancient story of Rebekah and Isaac, and the deep and lasting impression it has the power to make upon our minds, lies in the fact that it is more than just a tale of simple and artless romance leading to marriage. It is a divinely inspired record of historical fact; it is a supernaturally preserved love story which has unmistakable overtones that speak to us of Christ and His church; and it has a powerful application to twentieth century men and women.

THE BLESSING OF GOD

Before concluding our chapter we must take note of how this most arresting record opens and closes. It opens with the blessing of Abraham and it closes with the love of Isaac. (Gen. 24: 1, 67)The blessing of God and the love of Christ. Is anything more desired among Christians than the blessing of God? Is anything more engaging than the love of Christ? In our next chapter we shall consider the latter, but here let us ponder the blessing of God. Twice over the theme is referred to, first in relation to the sending of the nameless servant on his mission, and then in the fulfilling of that mission in the land and house of Laban. It is the special ministry of the Holy Spirit to reveal to us the blessing of the Lord. "For eye hath not seen nor ear heard, neither hath it entered into the heart of man the things that God hath prepared for them that love him, but He hath revealed them unto us by His Spirit." (1st Cor. 2: 9. 10)

Rebekah was given an earnest, a first instalment of that blessing which maketh rich. All his master's goods were in the servant's hand and he gave Rebekah a gold ring of half a shekel's weight and two bracelets for her wrists of ten shekels'weight of gold. In like manner we who have believed have been given an earnest of our inheritance in that we have been sealed by that Holy Spirit of promise. (Eph. 1: 13) In addition to all this a blessing rested upon Rebekah in the day she set her face towards Isaac. She was sent on her way with these words "be thou the mother of thousands of millions, and let thy seed possess the gate of them that hate them." (Gen. 24: 60)

The original idea behind having weddings in church buildings was not simply to provide a suitable backdrop for the occasion but that the couple might seek God's blessing upon their union. "For what dost thou make request?" was Elijah's parting word to his successor; Elisha made a good request. He asked not for fame nor wealth, but for a double portion of his master's spirit. (2nd Kings 2: 9) The double portion was the blessing reserved for the firstborn. The supreme thing must be the blessing of God. This is why in so many marriage ceremonies the Aaronic blessing is heard "The Lord bless thee, and keep thee; the Lord make His face to shine upon thee, and be gracious unto thee; the Lord lift up His countenance upon thee, and give thee peace." (Num. 6: 22-27) The people were just about to set out on their momentous journey from the plains of Sinai when the blessing was first pronounced. Happy indeed are they who desire above all God's blessing upon their union as they step out together upon married life.

•••

'And Laban said unto Jacob, Because thou art my brother, shouldst thou therefore serve me for nothing? Tell me, what shall thy wages be? And Laban had two daughters: the name of the elder was Leah, and the name of the younger was Rachel.

Leah was tender eyed; but Rachel was beautiful and well favoured. And Jacob loved Rachel; and said, I will serve thee seven years for Rachel thy younger daughter.

And Laban said, It is better that I give her to thee, than that I should give her to another man: abide with me.

And Jacob served seven years for Rachel; and they seemed unto him but a few days, for the love he had for her.'

~ From Genesis Chapter Twenty Nine

Jacob's Bride

"Many waters cannot quench love, neither can the floods drown it: if a man would give all the substance of his house for love, it would utterly be contemned." Song of Solomon 8 verse 7.

One of the most touching love stories in the whole Bible is that of Jacob winning the hand of Rachel. Away in the land of Laban, his mother's brother, and far from home, Jacob's affections rested upon Rachel, the younger sister of Leah and daughter of Laban. There was a heavy price to be paid. Jacob must serve seven years for Rachel. When the years were fulfilled, alas, Jacob was deceived, for Laban gave him Leah instead of Rachel. (Gen. 29: 25) Jacob protested, but Laban excused himself saying it was the custom of the country that the elder should marry first. It was then agreed that if Jacob would serve another seven years he could have Rachel's hand. This he did, and willingly, as the scripture indicates which says, "And Jacob served seven years for Rachel; and they seemed unto him but a few days, because of the love he had for her." In all the after light of the New Testament it is not difficult to see in this a most beautiful and expressive foreshadowing of how Christ won His Bride, the Church.

It may be argued that Rachel, the much loved wife of Jacob, and mother of Joseph and Benjamin, should more strictly be considered as a type of Israel. Certainly her last word was "Benoni" which means sorrowful; and Jeremiah pictured her as rising from the dead to weep over the children who were carried into the Babylonian captivity (Jer. 31 v. 15). This picture is viewed as being prophetic of the slaughter of the innocents by Herod at the time of our Lord's birth (Matt. 2 vs. 16-18). All this and much more seem to identify Rachel with the sorrows and tribulations of Israel, the elect nation. Nevertheless our purpose is to look at the brides of Genesis, and to consider them as being typical of the New Testament Church, the Body and the Bride of Christ. That we have warrant for doing so will become clear as we pursue our theme.

THE PERFECT NUMBER

In order to have the hand of Rachel, Jacob must take the servant's place, not for a year or two but for seven years, a period of time which testifies to the completeness of his devotion to her.

There are four perfect numbers in scripture. The number three signifies divine perfection as seen in the three persons of the Godhead. The ten commandments of the moral law mark the number ten as denoting moral perfection, while governmental perfection is the thought behind the number twelve. Our Lord anticipated a day when the twelve apostles would sit upon twelve thrones judging the twelve tribes of the children of Israel. (Matt. 19: 28)

Seven however, is probably the most prominent number found in scripture. It seems to stand for spiritual perfection or completeness. We read of the seven spirits before God's throne, probably a reference to the seven-fold spirit of Isaiah's prophecy. (Isa. 11: 2) The first direct mention of this number is in connection with creation week: "the Lord blessed the seventh day and sanctified it." (Gen. 2: 3) Take one day from a week or add one day to it and immediately its completeness is destroyed. A complete week is made up of just seven days and that for men of every religion and of none. Moses wrote that the days of man's years are "three-

score and ten" (Psa. 90: 10)or ten times seven. We are told
that in seven year cycles the human body undergoes certain
changes and we are also familiar with the "seven ages of
man."

It is quite remarkable how God dealt with His ancient
earthly people in cycles of seven and multiples of seven. 5
(Dan. 9: 24) In Israel there were weeks of days, weeks of
weeks, weeks of months and weeks of years. The multiplied
references would fill a book but they combine to identify the
number seven as a special number, a number of perfection
and completeness. The seven years that Jacob served for
Rachel stand forever as a memorial to the fulness of Jacob's
devotion to his bride. Indeed, whatever else might be said
of the doubling of the seven years, this much must be
conceded: Rachel was doubly assured that the one who had
won her hand was a man who loved her with all his heart.

THE TRUE SERVANT

To angels and devout men the condescension of the Son
of God is ever a subject of adoring wonder. He who was rich
became poor. (2nd Cor. 8: 9)The distance between these two
points is as far as the east is from the west. The Sovereign of
the universe became a servant and to Him in this character
the scriptures bear repeated testimony.

In four main passages Isaiah the prophet represents the
Lord Jesus as the Servant of Jehovah. (Isa. 42: 1-4) These passages are sometimes referred to as Isaiah's servant songs.
The first song gives us on overview of the Servant's mission.
It introduces the Servant, highlights His faithfulness, and
anticipates the completion of His purpose, which is to
accomplish salvation and to establish God's order upon the
earth. The second song calls attention to the apparent failure
of the Servant in His mission to the nation of Israel. It shows
however that while rejected by Israel, the Servant will bring
salvation to the Gentiles; and after that He will effect the
restoration of Israel to the land promised to them in the
covenant made with Abraham. In the third song the empha-

sis is upon the fact that the Servant's mission would be fulfilled through suffering and affliction. Out of all that He suffered has come that which ministers to our lasting good and blessing. The final song celebrates the vindication of Jehovah's Servant. After all He endured, both at the hands of men and at the hand of God, His days are prolonged. (The reference seems to be to the resurrection of Christ.) He sees His seed and the pleasure of the Lord prospers in His hand. (See Isa. 49: 1-4, 50: 1-6, 52: 13, 53: 12)

Of the four evangelists it is Mark who presents the Saviour in this character. He begins his report like no other. Passing over the genealogy of Christ he brings us immediately to His public ministry. 8 (Mark 1: 14) After all, it is not a servant's genealogy but his ministry that is of consequence. Mark begins with the Saviour working and ends with Him risen from the dead, but working still with the disciples He had just commissioned to carry the gospel to every creature. This is how Mark concludes the matter, "so then, after the Lord had spoken unto them, He was received up into heaven, and sat on the right hand of God. And they went forth, and preached everywhere, the Lord working with them, and confirming the word with signs following." (Mark 16: 20)

The key scripture on the servanthood of the Saviour must undoubtedly be the second chapter of the epistle to the Philippians. (Phil. 2: 5-11) Although in the form of God, our Lord Jesus Christ was found in fashion as a man. Again, He humbled Himself (note the voluntary nature of the act) and became obedient unto death, even the death of the cross. Before beginning the ministry of the upper room the Lord Jesus engaged in an act of service that wondrously illustrated the truth of His self-humbling. He laid aside His garments and took a towel and girded Himself. He then poured water into a basin and proceeded to wash the disciples' feet. Thus he performed the most menial task the eastern servant was called upon to perform. (John 13: 4, 5) One could be excused for thinking that Paul had that upper room scene before his mind when he wrote in Philippians what is considered by many the greatest Christological passage in the entire Bible. Thus Christ won His bride, by voluntarily taking the servant's place just as Jacob did to win the hand of Rachel.

MOVED BY LOVE

Scripture is very specific in spelling out what it was that moved Jacob to serve for Rachel, "It was because of the love he had for her." The New Testament was written in a language that had a remarkable capacity for setting forth the finer points of given ideas. The Greek language could express shades of meaning in words which in our language may mean many things. The word "love" is a notable example; it is used in modern English literally to cover a multitude of sins, as well as to express what is beautiful and noble. Several words in Greek represent love in its varied forms and aspects, but in the New Testament "AGAPE" is the word used to convey the Christian concept of love. Other words convey the idea of emotion of one kind or another, but "AGAPE" represents love as an attitude of heart and mind.

"AGAPE has to do with the mind: it is not simply an emotion which rises unbidden in our hearts; it is a principle by which we deliberately live. Agape has supremely to do with the will. It is a conquest, a victory, an achievement. No one ever naturally loved his enemies. To love one's enemies is a conquest of all our natural inclinations and emotions." (Barclay. New Testament Words P. 21) This is the word Paul used three times in Eph. 5 when discussing the love that husbands should have for their wives. It's true meaning is seen here in Jacob. True love has at its root the idea of self-sacrifice.

There is a beautiful story told in the book of Exodus about the Hebrew servant who had served the full seven year period in his master's house as required by the law. (Ex. 21: 2-6) During this time he had acquired a wife and children. He was now free to leave, but the law stated that he must go out alone. His wife and children would belong to his master. The story tells how he refused to go out free, committing himself instead to his master to be his servant forever.

The servant foregoing his personal freedom, revealed what was in his heart when he said, "I love my master." Having served the legal time he was perfectly free to go out. But what of his wife and his children? How could he leave them behind and at the same time enjoy his freedom? This is how he declared his love for them. He sacrificed his own personal freedom. He walked over to the door-post where in the presence of the judge his ear was pierced with an awl. Thereafter his wife and children could look upon that pierced ear and read in it powerful proof of a love that embraced them all.

On the evening of our Lord's resurrection He appeared to His disciples gathered together in the upper room, the doors being shut for fear of the Jews. He spoke peace to their troubled hearts and then He shewed them His hands and His feet. (Luke 24: 36-40) The message of the pierced hands and feet and of the pierced ear is one. It is a message that tells of love, imperishable love, love that proved itself in self-sacrifice. Of course we do not look today upon pierced ears or hands or feet, but in the communion service we gaze upon bread broken and wine poured out; but the message is just the same, a message that tells of love that counts not the cost in terms of expending itself for the sake of its object. And it has ever been like that: true love gives itself and always puts its object first. Jacob's commitment to Rachel was like that. For her sake he gave himself in willing service. What a beautiful foreshadowing we have in this of what it was that moved the Saviour to take the servant's place that He might win the Church. Lest there should be any doubt, Paul affirms in Ephesians that "Christ loved the Church and gave Himself for it." (Eph. 5: 15)

LOVE EXTRAORDINARY

Had Jacob simply served seven years, that would have

been ordinary and according to custom, but the added seven years gave his love an extra dimension and marked it out as extraordinary love. Such is the love of Christ. Many years later when Jonathan died, David remembered his love and lamented over him and said, "Your love to me was wonderful, passing the love of women. (2nd Sam. 1: 26) It is probable that David had in mind the women who lined the streets upon his return after the defeat of Goliath. How their hearts went out to the victor as they cheered him on his way. But theirs was a kind of hero love and it soon waned. Jonathan's love was of a different and superior order, it had about it the quality of constancy, it was not susceptible to the winds of change. The love of Christ is like that. In its length and breadth and depth and height, it is a love that passes knowledge; and it is our constant theme who are members together of that Church which is destined to become His Bride.

Christ's love is a love from which there is no separation: "For I am persuaded, that neither death, nor life, nor angels, nor principalities, nor powers, nor things present, nor things to come, nor height, nor depth, nor any other creature, shall be able to separate us from the love of God, which is in Christ Jesus our Lord." (Rom. 8: 38, 39) This is the kind of love described by Paul to the Christians at Corinth: Love that suffereth long, and is kind; love that envieth not; love that vaunteth not itself and is not puffed up. Love that doth not behave itself unseemly, that seeketh not her own, that is not easily provoked and that thinketh no evil; Love that rejoiceth not in iniquity, but rejoiceth in the truth; That beareth all things, believeth all things, hopeth all things, endureth all things. (1st Cor. 13: 4-7) Such is the quality of true love, and only such love can bind two lives together in a bond that nothing short of death will be able to break.

LOVE'S CONSTANCY

And old proverb says "hope deferred makes the heart grow faint." This was not the case, however, in the matter of

Jacob's love for Rachel. Although he served the stated seven years twice over it is recorded that the multiplied years seemed as just a few days because of the love he had for her. The love of Christ is an everlasting love taking its character from the great lover himself. When it says therefore that Christ loved the Church and gave himself for it, we believe that if it were necessary - blessed be God it is not, but if it were - He would do all over again today what He did two thousand years ago when He loved the Church and gave Himself for it. This is the grand thing about the love of Christ. It encompasses the entire spectrum of our experience. He loved us, He loves us still and He will love us yet for His love knows no end.

When Jesus came into the world it was recorded of him, that "the Son of Man came not to be ministered unto but to minister and to give His life a ransom for many." (Matt. 20: 28) Note carefully the two things He came to do, to minister and to give. What a pattern for all and especially for those who come to pledge their troth to each other: they come to serve and to give. Even now our Lord engages in wonderful service on the behalf of His people. He is in the presence of God for us. He is occupied there as the representative and High Priest of His people. He never wearies, for He ever lives to make intercession for us. (Hebs. 7: 25)

Perhaps the most marvellous thing of all is that when He comes again in the fulness of His glory, even then He shall gird Himself and make us sit down to eat and He will come forth and serve us. (Luke 12: 37) We could scarcely believe this were it not so clearly stated in God's word, and the scripture cannot be broken. This greatest of lovers, the lover of our souls, delights to engage in the service of His loved ones. He serves us now, in this the time of His rejection, and He will serve us then in His kingdom. Jacob's love for Rachel was just as steadfast in adversity as it had been in days of promise and prosperity.

The discovery of how he had been deceived by Laban at the end of the seven years must have been an occasion of extreme disappointment and frustration for Jacob. Had he been overwhelmed by bitterness we could certainly have sympathised with him. Another power controlled him however, and enabled him in that dark hour not only to survive but to overcome. It was the power of his affection for Rachel.

In Solomon's Song we read, "many waters cannot quench love, neither can the floods drown it." (Song of S. 8: 7) Jacob's love for Rachel was proof of this, but the supreme proof is found in the cross, for greater love has no man than this, that a man should lay down his life for his friends, (John 15: 13) and yet it was while we were still sinners that Christ died for us. It is not for nothing that the marriage ceremony presupposes a love that will abide in sickness and in health, in joy and in sorrow, in prosperity and in adversity.

A depressing feature of today's society is a manifest departure from this ideal. The increasing numbers of marriages ending in divorce is putting at risk the very fabric of society itself; and an alarming feature of all this is that the slightest provocation seems to serve, as an acceptable pretext, for the dissolution of the union. In addition, many seem to think the simple formalisation of their relationship such an unnecessary encumbrance that they decide to come together without being married at all. Indeed we are told that this saves a great deal of trouble should there come a parting of the ways. In reality, of course, it only reflects the absence of the most basic element in true love, namely commitment and loyalty. To say that such relationships are based on love is a caricature of the very nature of love and an abandonment of even the pretence of a love that takes its character from Christ's love for the Church. On the other hand a marriage contracted in a spirit of humility begotten of true love will usually prove a permanent and happy union. There must first be commitment such as is seen in Jacob and supremely in Jesus. Then the union will deepen and the marriage will be enriched.

LOVE THE ONLY GROUND

Quite clearly a very deep affection entered into the relationship between Jacob and Rachel. The bond between them was well grounded in love, love that was pure and simple. It might be argued, however falsely, that Isaac's bride had been attracted by great possessions since all his master's goods were in the hands of Abraham's servant and he gave to Rebekah jewels and bracelets of gold at their first meeting and later spoke of the way in which his master had been blessed. Or it might be thought in our next chapter, that Joseph's bride had been attracted by great position, for after all, Joseph had been placed second only to the king upon his throne. One thing is clear, no such thoughts entered into this relationship. Jacob had nothing of position or of possession. It was the love he had for her that called forth from Rachel the deepest affection for him. This was no marriage of convenience, nor did material considerations enter into this relationship. On the contrary it rested upon a love that causes us to think of Jesus' love, a love of which the apostle of love wrote, "we love Him, because He first loved us." (1st John 4: 19)

We need to ponder more and more the love of Christ, for so a new dimension will be added to all our associations. Our family relationships and our assembly fellowships will, as a result, be elevated to a new and higher plane and more and more we shall know that motivation so beautifully expressed by Paul when he said, "the love of Christ constraineth us." (2nd Cor. 5: 14) Love is the superlative characteristic of Christianity. Jesus said, "By this shall all men know that you are my disciples if ye have love one toward another." (John 13: 35) It was in the context of great protestations of loyalty that Simon Peter failed so miserably. He denied his Lord, not once or twice but three times, and he did so with oaths and curses. It is noteworthy that on the occasion of the post-resurrection encounter Christ had with his erring servant, He did not challenge Peter's original sincerity nor did He examine his grasp of doctrine, important as both these things are. He rather raised the issue that is central to all issues, the issue of the heart. He sought a heart renewed in love and loyalty to Himself, and finding it, He commanded Peter to prove that love by feeding the sheep and tending the lambs of Christ's flock. (John 21: 15) True love for the Lord is seen in love for His people. This will manifest itself in a readiness to serve one another.

"I love the Lord" (Psa. 116: 1) declared the Psalmist and in doing so he wrote the bottom line of godly testimony through the ages. Too often the common bond is nothing more than a common antagonism towards some third person, or a mutual sympathy with some cherished prejudice; whereas it ought to be a common love for Christ. We must give more earnest heed to the Saviour's exhortation, when having displayed His love by washing His disciples' feet on the occasion already referred to, He said, "I have given you an example that you should do as I have done." (John 13: 15) Truly a baptism of this kind of love would revitalise many a family, and revive many an assembly, and restore to us something of the divine ideal, often so painfully missing today.

•••

'And Pharaoh said unto Joseph, Forasmuch as God hath shown thee all
this, there is none so discreet and wise as thou art:
Thou shalt be over my house, and according unto thy word shall all my
people be ruled: only in the throne will I be greater than thou.
And Pharaoh said unto Joseph, See, I have set thee over all the land of
Egypt.
And Pharaoh took off his ring from his hand, and put it upon Joseph's
hand, and arrayed him in vestures of fine linen, and put a gold chain
about his neck;
And he made him to ride in the second chariot which he had; and they
cried before him, Bow the knee: and he made him ruler over all the land
of Egypt.
And Pharaoh said unto Joseph, I am Pharaoh, and without thee shall no
man lift up his hand or foot in all the land of Egypt.
And Pharaoh called Joseph's name Zaphanath-paaneah; and gave him
as his wife Asenath the daughter of Potipherah priest of On. And Joseph
went out over all the land of Egypt.'

~ From Genesis Chapter Forty One

Joseph's Bride

"The marriage of the Lamb is come and his wife has made herself ready." Rev. 19 v. 7.

If the first bride of Genesis is Eve then the last is Asenath who was given to Joseph in the day of his glory in Egypt. Asenath is just one of several persons of whom we read who were born outside the circle of the elect race, but who were introduced into it through remarkable circumstances. Rahab and Ruth and Naaman were others. These combine to teach us that whereas election is undoubtedly a corporate truth, salvation is always an individual matter. Failure to appreciate this had led many to unwarranted extremes.

Jesus said, "I am the door: by me if any man enter in he shall be saved." (John 10: 9) The woman of Canaan whose daughter was grievously vexed with a devil, had no claims upon the Son of David, for he was not sent but to the lost sheep of the house of Israel. But when she recognised her true position and took her true ground and cried out "Lord, help me," there was the immediate response, "O woman great is your faith, be it unto you even as you will." And her daughter was made whole from that very hour. (Matt. 15: 28) It was the same with the centurion whose servant was at the point of death (See Luke 7: 1-10) and it is just the same today; the Lord Jesus delights to honour the faith of all who call upon Him and "whosoever shall call upon the name of the Lord shall be saved." (Rom. 10: 15)

JOSEPH....JESUS

Of the very many men in the Old Testament scriptures who typify the Lord Jesus, probably the most outstanding is Joseph. For one thing, nothing is recorded against Joseph, and we can never forget how Jesus said to His accusers, "which of you convinces me of sin?" (John 8: 46) Even Pilate's wife urged her husband to have nothing to do with this just man; (Matt. 29: 19) and the penitent who was crucified with Him declared, "this man has done nothing amiss;" (Luke 23: 41) while the centurion in charge of the soldiers that day boldly announced, "this was a righteous man." (Luke 23: 48) Truly Jesus fully magnified the law and made it honourable. (Isa. 42: 21)

Every detail of Joseph's life breathes the spirit of Jesus. The coat of many colours given to him in token of his father's love reminds us of those occasions when the silence of the heavens was broken, by the audible voice of His Father in heaven bearing witness to the Lord Jesus and saying "This is my beloved Son in whom I am well pleased." (Matt. 3: 17) Twice, in figure, Joseph went down into death. First, suffering at the hand of his brothers he went down into the pit, and then suffering at the hands of the Egyptians, he went down into prison. In a peculiar way these two experiences seem to illustrate how Jew and Gentile conspired together to put Jesus to death.

Isaac typifies Christ as the Son, Jacob as the servant, but Joseph sets Him forth as the Saviour. Joseph was the means of deliverance for the butler in the prison, he accomplished deliverance for the whole land of Egypt, and he was God's instrument in the preservation of the family to which he belonged. Joseph, therefore, might be said to represent the Lord Jesus, first as a personal Saviour, then as the Saviour of the world and finally in a coming day as the Saviour of His people Israel. In his going down into the prison on the one hand, and in his being brought up again out of the prison to stand before Pharaoh on the other, we have no difficulty in seeing the Lord Jesus, both in His death and resurrection.

THIS DAY....THAT DAY

Another day however, is envisaged in our scripture. It is a day of glory, the day when the Saviour shall come again, in all the glory of His second advent, "to be glorified in His saints and to be admired in all them that believe." (2nd Thess. 1: 10) Now the glorification of the Crucified must be understood in a two-fold way. He is glorified today at God's right hand. Peter made this clear in his sermon at Pentecost, when he said, "this Jesus has God raised up, whereof we all are witnesses. Therefore being by the right hand of God exalted, and having received of the Father the promise of the Holy Ghost, he hath shed forth this, which you now see and hear. For David is not ascended into the heavens; but he said himself, the Lord said unto my Lord, sit on my right hand, until I make your foes your footstool. Therefore let all the house of Israel know assuredly, that God has made that same Jesus, whom you have crucified, both Lord and Christ." (Acts 2: 32-36)

In His letter to the church at Laodicea the risen Lord himself gave this assurance and pledge to the overcomer, "to him that overcomes will I grant to sit with me on my throne, even as I also overcame and am sat down with my Father in His throne." (Rev. 3: 21)

He fills the throne, the throne above
He fills it without wrong.
The object of His Father's love
The theme of angels song.

All this however, is not obvious in this age; it is a private rather than a public matter. But a day will come when what is now true in heaven and in the hearts of all who love Him will become manifest throughout the entire universe. These two aspects of Christ's glorification are linked together by Paul in what we have already called one of the greatest Christological passages anywhere in scripture. He says, "God has highly exalted Him and given Him a name that is above every name." That is true at this present moment. But then he anticipates the day of Christ's appearing, when His glory will be publicly revealed, and he adds, "that at the name of Jesus every knee should bow of things in heaven and things on earth and things under the earth and that every tongue should confess that Jesus Christ is Lord to the glory of God the Father." (Phil. 2: 11) It is that coming day that is so wondrously illustrated in the day of Joseph's glory in Egypt.

Note the characteristics of that day:

(1) Highly Exalted

Pharaoh said to Joseph, "see I have set you over all the land of Egypt." Thus Joseph was made ruler over all Egypt and to emphasise the point Pharaoh decreed that no man might lift up hand or foot without Joseph's authority. The contrast between being Pharaoh's prisoner and being his prime minister is difficult for us at this distance to comprehend. In the same way we are unable to measure the self-humbling of our Saviour, who was rich yet for our sakes became poor. Nor can we imagine that upward step from "the death of the Cross" to His present highly exalted position. Even now our Lord Jesus Christ is exalted higher than the heavens, but in the day of His appearing God will make His glory known to all, "for every eye shall see Him, and they also that pierced Him: and all kindreds of the earth shall wail because of Him." (Rev. 1: 7)

(2) Glorified

The ring transferred from the hand of Pharaoh to the hand of Joseph, the vestures of fine linen and the gold chain about his neck are all emblems of glory. In them one can almost hear an echo of the Lord's prayer, "for thine is the kingdom, the power and the glory." Both the type and the prayer will find their full expression when Jesus comes in all the glory of His second advent, for then there shall be one king over all the earth and His Name one. In that day Isaiah's ancient prophecy will be fulfilled which says, "Behold a king shall reign in righteousness and princes shall rule in judgment." (Isa. 32: 1)

The subject of clothing is very prominent in scripture, from the aprons of fig leaves in the garden of Eden, to the robe of righteousness and the garment of salvation. Many books have been written on the garments of Israel's High Priest; and much has been made of the garments of Jesus. What shall we say of Joseph's garments? The coat of many colours was his as the beloved son; the coat he left when he fled from the intrigues of Potiphar's wife was his as the perfect servant. But now we see him adorned in glorious raiment, the token of Joseph as the exalted Lord.

(3) Proclaimed Lord of All

Wherever Joseph was found in that day a cry went before him. A cry simple and yet profound, "Bow the knee." We cannot fail to read in that cry Paul's triumphant assertion "Every knee shall bow and every tongue confess that Jesus Christ is Lord." Of course He always was Lord, for even at the time of His birth the angelic announcement was of "a Saviour which is Christ the Lord." (Luke 2: 11) He is repeatedly referred to as such throughout the gospel narratives and in His death the penitent thief cried out and said, "Lord remember me." But now He is Lord in a new and added sense for we read, "to this end He died and rose and revived that He might be Lord both of the dead and the living." (Rom. 14: 9) His Lordship is indeed universal for "He is Lord of all" and yet His people speak of Him as "our Lord", for Lordship represents a special relationship between Christ and His people.

We who love Him gladly acknowledge Him even now, "our Lord and our God," but then all things in heaven and upon the earth and under the earth will bow before Him and recognise that "He is Lord" who today is still despised and rejected of men.

(4) Given a Name

Zaphnath-paaneah was the name given to Joseph in the day of his glory in Egypt. This hyphenated name has a dual meaning. It means (i) the revealer of secrets and (ii) the Saviour of the world. The woman of Samaria found the Lord Jesus able both to reveal the secrets of her heart and at the same time to redeem her from all iniquity. Hence her testimony, "Come and see a man that told me all things that ever I did: is not this the Christ." (John 4: 29) To which her hearers replied"....this is indeed the Christ, the Saviour of the World." (John 4: 42) At the time of His first advent the angel said "call His name Jesus for He shall save His people from their sins." (Matt. 1: 21) Alas He passed through this world unrecognised, save by a few, and then He was taken and by wicked hands nailed to the accursed tree. Proud sinners set that precious name at naught for they wrote over His cross the inscription, "This is Jesus." (Matt. 27: 37) But in the day of His glory He will be proclaimed the universal Lord and that in the very scene of His rejection. In that day when God will set His King upon His holy hill of Zion, He will simply announce, "this is Jesus" and at the very mention of that Name every knee shall bow. (Psa. 2: 6)

> *Jesus, Oh how sweet the Name;*
> *Jesus every day the same;*
> *Jesus let all saints proclaim*
> *His worthy Name for ever.*

....THE WEDDING DAY

Now it was precisely at that point, the day of his glory in Egypt, that Joseph received his bride. Her name was Asenath and like the other brides of Genesis she wonderfully pictures the Church. We have seen how Eve was created to share with Adam the headship of the entire creation. Eve points forward to the destiny of the church which is to reign with Christ, when all things in heaven and on earth are gathered together in one under Him. Rebekah speaks of the church in the counsels of the Father's heart concerning His Son and then sought and brought into union with Christ; while it is the Church's identification with Christ in this present season of His rejection that is seen in Rachel sharing with Jacob the time of his exile from home. But Asenath anticipates the wedding day. This is the great thing to be borne in mind when thinking of Asenath.

There are three terms used of the church in the New Testament that need to be carefully distinguished.

(i) A Virgin   2 Cor. 11: 2
(ii) A Bride   Rev. 2:9
(iii) A Wife   Rev. 19:7

These three terms may well derive from the three-fold pattern of the oriental marriage. There was first the betrothal which was a legally binding affair, then the coming of the bridegroom and finally the marriage feast.

Today and throughout this age of the Saviour's absence, the church is viewed as "a virgin espoused to one man" even to Christ. On the part of the church corporately and each member of it individually, what is called for now is fidelity and faithfulness to the person of Christ. Then in that day when Christ is revealed in power and great glory, the virgin will become the bride, for the church will be presented to Him as a glorious church, His spotless bride, and, "When Christ who is our life shall appear then shall we also appear with Him in glory."(Col. 3: 4) Finally, throughout the reign of Christ the bride will be "the Lamb's wife." His consort upon His throne, and His partner by His side. And so when "Jesus shall reign where'er the sun doth its successive journey run" we shall reign with Him for so shall we ever be with the Lord.

Mid the splendours of the glory
Which we hope ere long to share
Christ our head and we His members
Shall appear divinely fair.

Asenath represents the church in the second of these designations. In Asenath we see the Church as a bride adorned for her husband.

....AND OTHER DAYS

It is true that a bride is a bride only for a day and how quickly that day passes. But when the festivities are over and the guests are departed and the wedding dress is laid aside, the vows that were made still stand. Making vows in any context is exceedingly serious. It is better not to vow, than to vow and not pay. In the marriage service both bride and groom make the most solemn vows to each other "in the presence of God," and before invited and appointed witnesses. How sad it is, that after so short a time, in so many cases, the wedding day vows seem to be forgotten.

One of the finest tributes that any of us can pay to others is to say that their word is their bond. The claim is repeatedly made in the scriptures that "God is faithful."(1st Cor. 10: 13) The meaning of this is that God is true to His word. Multiplied references could be cited in proof of this aspect of the character of God. Indeed the proof of this has been built into nature itself, "God is not mocked: for whatsoever a man sows, that shall he also reap." (Gal. 6: 7) Since faithfulness in God is faithfulness to His word, it follows that faithfulness in man means the very same thing. The marriage vows therefore must not be made lightly; for they pledge the most solemn faithfulness of each partner to the other.

THE DIFFICULT TIMES

Joseph and Asenath would have every married couple remember the day when before God and in the presence of all His people they pledged their troth each to the other, to have and to hold from that day forward, for better for worse, for richer for poorer, in sickness and in health... The reality certainly is that life in general and married life in particular is cast in the context of these extremes. Without a moment's hesitation we can say that Joseph carried into his marriage to Asenath, as a deep seated conviction, the knowledge that life is not all plain sailing and clear skies. Joseph's pathway up to the throne in Egypt was one of suffering and affliction. He had been betrayed by his brethren and sold into the hands of the Gentiles. He was falsely accused as Potiphar's steward and as a consequence was cast into prison. Even there he had been cruelly forgotten by the one he had so wonderfully befriended. Joseph's conviction had been hammered out on the anvil of personal experience.

Through all the vicissitudes of his life Joseph had come to an acknowledgement of God's ways. He had learned that through all these difficulties God was doing something in him. He was in fact, preparing him to share the throne of Egypt. This is a matter of great significance in married life, and here again, the pattern for us is Christ and the Church. Our Lord's pathway in this world was also one of suffering and affliction. He was a man of sorrows and acquainted with grief. (Isa. 53: 3) Because of that, He is able now to exercise His present ministry in heaven as the High Priest of His people. He is there as one who is personally acquainted with our infirmities. (See Hebs. 4: 15) Moreover the experience of the Church of Christ is one of suffering and affliction as well. The Lord Himself prepared us for this when He said "in the world you shall have tribulation but be of good cheer for I have overcome the world." (John 16: 23) Just as at any given moment the tide is in at one part and out at another so the history of the Church has been one of suffering. If this has not been very marked in one place it has been in another.

In the day of his marriage to Asenath Joseph knew these things. He understood that the problems which must inevitably arise are not in themselves so important: it is our reaction to them that is vital. He may not always have seen it at the time but afterwards Joseph came to realise that however dark the day had been, all the while, the Lord who has established His throne in the heavens and whose kingdom rules over all, was causing all things, even in Joseph's life, to work together for good. He acknowledged this quite openly, when his brothers, with shame upon their faces, stood before him, fearful lest Joseph would at the last exact vengeance upon them for their earlier treatment of him. His actual words were "You meant it for evil, but God overruled it for good." (Gen. 50: 20)

When two distinct personalities are fused together in the bond of marriage there is bound to be friction from time to time and especially in the initial stages of the marriage. Some of the testings will be provoked by the perverseness of our own petty thinking and must be recognised for what they are. But then other matters will arise, matters for which we are wholly unprepared, problems that seem insoluble, obstacles that appear insurmountable. Issues may arise that would even seem to threaten the integrity of the marriage itself. In such situations we must stand upon the same ground as Joseph and dare to believe that the living God who is working all things after the counsel of His own will is at work in our lives too. It is ours to wait together upon the Lord and we shall surely find

> *The bud may have a bitter taste*
> *But sweet will be the flower.*

The old adage says, the family that prays together stays together. Certainly husbands and wives should pray together before retiring every night. They should pray out loud in each other's presence. Two benefits will flow from this exercise: they will be able to see their problems more objectively and they will almost certainly become of one mind as to their reaction to these same problems. Why did Simon Peter in the midst of the storm on the lake, ask to come to Jesus walking on the water? Was it not because he believed, that in the presence of such a storm, the best place for him was to be as near to the Lord as possible? Husbands and wives who react aright to the difficult times will discover that afterward these very experiences will yield the peaceable fruits of righteousness and will minister to the enrichment of their marriage.

THE PAST AND THE FUTURE

It is noteworthy that attention is called in our scripture not only to Asenath's future but also to her past. She was the daughter of Potipherah the priest of On. Three times she is said to have been the daughter of Potipherah who is believed to have officiated in the Great Temple of the Sun at Heliopolis not far from modern Cairo. What a remarkable contrast, from being the daughter of the priest of the Sun worshippers of On, to being the wife of Joseph, the most notable type of Christ in scripture. True believers, who form the Church are not ignorant of their past. Writing to the Ephesians, Paul contrasts what they were "by nature" and what they now are "by grace:" "by nature the children of wrath, even as others. But God who is rich in mercy, for His great love wherewith He loved us, even when we were dead in sins, has quickened us together with Christ, (by grace ye are saved)." (Eph. 2: 1-5)

The epistle to the Ephesians is perhaps the fullest exposition we have in the New Testament of the exalted position the saved occupy in virtue of their association with Christ. Salvation here is shown to be more than deliverance from sin and wrath. The saved are raised up together and made to sit together in heavenly places in Christ. In Him they are blessed with all spiritual blessings and sealed with that Holy Spirit of promise which is the earnest or guarantee of the inheritance.

All this is surely foreshadowed in the new position Asenath was introduced to through her union with Joseph. Even the silence of scripture at this point is worthy of note, for we read nothing of Asenath's own works. She is given by Pharaoh to Joseph, who takes her as his bride; Asenath herself is wholly passive. Even so, the present position of all who are in Christ and their future prospects are wholly unrelated to their own efforts. If, for instance, we could attain heaven by human merit, heaven would soon become a veritable hell. But no, says Paul, "it is not of works lest any man should boast," (Eph. 2: 8, 9) it is by grace we are saved through faith, faith alone in Christ alone. But grace has not only saved us, grace has kept us, and the same grace will keep us until that day when we shall be presented faultless before the presence of His glory with exceeding joy. (Jude 24)

Scripture is also remarkably silent about Asenath's activity after her marriage to Joseph. Apart from being the mother of his children we know nothing of the role Asenath played in the unfolding drama of Joseph's life. It might not therefore be out of place to ask, what was God's will for Asenath who had now become the wife of Joseph? We have already considered this question in relation to Eve. The answer here is the same. In the context of Christian marriage the first duty of the wife is to support her husband in the outworking of God's will for his life. This does not mean that the woman cannot pursue a vocation different from that of her partner, but it does mean that the marriage bond is a union of such a character that one partner does not have a purpose in life independent of the other. Rather they walk together in subjection to the ultimate headship of Christ and together they seek to realise His will who works in us, both to will and to do of His good pleasure. (Phil. 2: 13)

A MOTHER IN ISRAEL

But we must not pass over too lightly the fact that Asenath was the mother of Joseph's two sons Ephraim and Manasseh. Evidently Joseph was much comforted by them as might be seen in the very names by which he called them - Ephraim means "to forget" and Manasseh means "to add". Through these two boys Joseph was helped to "forget those things that were behind and to reach forth unto those things that were before." (Phil. 3: 13).   Later the tribe of Joseph was divided into the two half tribes of Ephraim and Manasseh. These then took their place among the tribes to make up the number when the tribe of Levi was set apart for special service. Asenath's name consequently occupies an honoured place in the imperishable records of holy scripture. Her honour derives not only from her union with Joseph but also from the fact that her sons came to be numbered in so signal a manner with the people of God. Mary the mother of our Lord was "blessed" among women. Asenath too was blessed and every mother is blessed who sees her offspring walking in the ways of the Lord and seeking the honour of His name. In this Asenath's heart found its true fulfilment.

It is surely quite striking then that whereas we read a great deal concerning the three brides already considered, we read of Asenath only on her wedding day. This peculiar silence tends to confirm the view that the marriage of Joseph and Asenath anticipates the marriage of the Lamb when the Church will be presented to Christ. That is what we must ever keep before us. Like a modern bride in sight of the wedding day, every decision made and every duty undertaken somehow derives a certain significance from and bears a certain relation to the happy day in prospect, and what preparation, what careful planning of detail is made by the eager bride in anticipation of that day. And then when the day dawns, how quickly the fears and the frustrations are forgotten in the joy of the wedding feast. If we would keep our present experience in perspective we must never lose sight of the wedding day. Our comfort lies in the knowledge that our light affliction which is but for a moment, worketh for us a far more exceeding and eternal weight of glory. (2nd Cor. 4: 17)

•••

The Christian Home

"These words which I command thee this day, shall be in thine heart; and thou shalt teach them diligently unto thy children...." Deut 6: 6, 7.

When in the beginning God established human society, He built it upon the basis of the family unit, at the centre of which is the marriage bond. Anything that weakens that bond undermines the family unit and must ultimately be a blow struck against society itself. To say that today's society has long since moved away from the principles enshrined in the first marriage is only to state the obvious. In so much of the legislation being passed through the various assemblies of the western world, the cry is for equality, equal rights, equal pay for equal work, etc. etc. On the face of it, all this seems fair but the subtle effect of it is to move society away from its divinely appointed basis, i.e. the family unit, and on to another basis, i.e. the individual. Any society is only the aggregate of its families; and at any given time the condition of that society is just a reflection of the state of its family life.

The biblical position is that the family unit is the key to an integrated society. The family unit, built upon the marriage union, as instituted by the Creator, with the husband as the breadwinner, and the wife as the homemaker, is a concept that has served us well over a very long time, and should not be lightly cast aside by this generation. However, the pressures of modern society upon men, and especially upon women, to conform are almost overwhelming.

It is well understood that in civilised lands the legal process must always be kept under review; imbalances and anomalies will manifest themselves and these must be corrected. But when the balance swings, as it now seems to have done, so that the integrity of family life is being discounted then our legislators must urgently review the situation. The reality is that society is already paying a fearful price for this departure in terms of broken marriages and shattered homes, not to speak of such knock-on effects as the appalling increase in child abuse already referred to. The official statistics make heavy reading indeed. All who would live for God in this present evil world must beware; we must look to ourselves, to our families, and to our assemblies, lest the spirit abroad in the world should take root among us. We must be governed by what is of God, and according to His word, and by what is for His glory.

THE MARRIAGE BOND

God says in His word, "marriage is honourable in all." (Hebs. 13: 4) Even where the marriage is not a Christian marriage it is still to be prized, for that is what honourable means. The word is used of the reputation, acquired by a scholar of his being eminent in his field. It is translated elsewhere by the word "precious" and is used of the "precious blood of Christ" (1st Pet. 1: 18, 19) and of the "precious promises of God." (2nd Pet. 1: 4) Marriage as an institution should be held in reputation and esteemed very highly because God himself speaks of it as being honourable.

The triune God has emphatically set His seal to the marriage bond. God the Father instituted it at the dawn of creation and said, "for this cause shall a man leave his father and his mother and shall be joined unto his wife and they shall be one flesh." (Matt. 19: 5) God the Son sanctified marriage by His presence and by His words and His works at the marriage in Cana of Galilee where His first miracle was performed. (John 2: 1-11) And God the Holy Spirit placed His seal on the marriage relationship when He used it as a type of the sacred union that exists between Christ and His Church. (Eph. 5: 32) It flows from all this that our own happiness as well as God's blessing and society's health are all bound up in a proper view of marriage. The idea of a man and a woman being joined together in matrimony, and establishing a home which will be a decidedly Christian home is not an outmoded notion; it is something that is vitally relevant in today's society. In addition we cannot be indifferent to a matter that affects so deeply our own well-being and the well-being of our children.

THE CHRISTIAN HOME

The recovery of the concept of the Christian home should exercise the minds of Christian leaders to a far greater degree than at present. Preachers and teachers of the word of God should lay far greater stress upon this vital institution. The place given in scripture, to what we call the Christian home, is second only to that given to the ordering of the house of God.

Materialism has cultivated the image of the ideal home as a commodious place, well endowed with modern conveniences and stylish luxuries and of course, located in a fairly prestigious environment. All of this, is a question of degree, and those who have attained to it beyond the measure of most seem most ready to acknowledge, that nothing of this can satisfy the heart. Newly weds are naturally concerned about where they shall live. And yet it is not where we live, but how we live, that is supremely important: "man shall not live by bread alone, but by every word that proceeds out of the mouth of God." (Matt. 4: 4) We must begin by bringing our homes under the authority of the word of God. The advice of the mother of Jesus has lost none of its wisdom though spoken so long ago: "Whatsoever He says unto you, do it." (John 2: 5)

Christian homes will be like the house of Obed-Edom

who found room for the ark of the covenant which speaks so eloquently of the person and the presence of the Lord Jesus. They will also have a definite motto, one that encapsulates a real purpose in life, such as Joshua had when he said "as for me and my house, we will serve the Lord." (Joshua 24: 15)

Christian parents should consider how their homes can become more distinctively a Christian home. The achievement of this should be viewed as a process. We must be careful not to go to extremes. We live, by the will of God, in a world that is sinful and corrupt; and we shall remain in this environment until the Lord takes us out of it. In the meantime we should aim that the home is as an anteroom of heaven. This will require the careful exclusion of harmful programmes and periodicals. What spiritual grace there is, will be dissipated by the uncontrolled use of television and radio, and by the ready availability of improper literature which is around in such abundance today. The principle is that if good fruits are to be cultivated, then bad weeds must be restrained.

And yet while these things are vital the Christian home is more than all the negatives. There are essential positive steps that need to be taken, if our homes are to be brought within the range of what might reasonably be called the Christian home.

THE FAMILY ALTAR

The first thing that needs to be established is the family altar. For this the father should accept responsibility. He should ensure a family gathering for the reading of God's word on a daily, or at the outside, a weekly basis. He may read the scripture portion himself or invite his wife to read it in turn, or better still the whole family may participate in the reading.

In many so-called Christian homes the word of God is seldom opened; this is a sorrowful indictment of Christian fathers. Many parents in later years have confessed their regret at the neglect of this simple provision; which in a quiet way raises a standard within the family, and identifies the home as a Christian home in the minds of the children.

Believers universally accept that every good and every perfect gift comes from above, from the Father of lights with whom is no changeableness, and yet sadly, all too often day passes day and week passes week, without any open acknowledgement of this in the citadel of the Christian home.

Parents sometimes excuse themselves by saying that they are not given to praying in public and are therefore too self-conscious to engage in family prayer. But the exercise need not be a lengthy one, and the simple duty of reading a few verses of scripture, and of breathing a few sentences invoking God's blessing upon one's nearest and dearest is something for which God Himself will give grace, if it is approached in the spirit of Paul's assertion, "I can do all things through Christ who strengthens me." (Phil. 4: 13)

A poster that appeared on many bill-boards throughout Britain a few years ago asked the question, "Have you read the Bible today?" The implication was that daily Bible reading should be the habit of every person. Certainly Christians know that to maintain freshness in their spiritual experience they need a daily diet of prayer and the word of God. If this is true in the personal realm why should it be thought unnecessary in the domestic circle? A question mark must hang over the profession of any individual who neglects these provisions for his spiritual prosperity; and it is doubtful if a home that is not sanctified by the word of God and prayer can in any meaningful sense be considered a Christian home.

The practical consequence of this is, not just benefit for the children, but for the parents as well. They will find it necessary to keep their own lives under review so that the Bible is read, not just like a school reading book, but that its truth is seen by the children worked out in the daily habits and life-style of their parents. The family altar certainly calls for discipline, not only in terms of time and in the ordering of the household, but also and perhaps most importantly in the lives of the parents. This in turn will instil into the children a sense of self-discipline, the absence of which is having such a pernicious effect upon society today.

When God caused the punitive plagues to fall upon Egypt, one of them was the plague of darkness. It is described as a darkness that could be felt. The inspired record however says that God's people had 'light in their dwellings' (Ex. 10: 21-23) It is imperative that there is a clear shining of the light of God's word in our homes; and so much more as the darkness around us grows deeper.

A glory guilds the sacred page,
Majestic, as the sun;
It gives a light to every age;
It gives, but borrows none.

CHRISTIAN MOTHERS

Another factor is the mother's role in the home. Modern gadgetry has undoubtedly dealt with many of the chores, but has this resulted in mothers spending more time with their children? Christian mothers should think very carefully before delegating to others the care and upbringing of their children, especially when they are still of tender and very impressionable years - years that are critical to the development and direction of the child's later life.

The priceless influence of godly mothers upon their children is highlighted in scripture by reference to three of the most notable men who stood for God in their respective generations. Where did Moses learn of the greater riches than all the treasures of Egypt? (Hebs. 11: 26) Surely it was at his mother's knee. Samuel became a man of prayer, a man to whom the whole nation, in its distress, turned with this request, "pray for us." He could sincerely reply, "God forbid that I should sin against the Lord in ceasing to pray for you." (1st Sam. 12: 23) Will anyone deny a parallel between what Samuel became and what his mother had been?

Hannah was a woman of prayer, indeed Samuel was born in answer to his mother's prayers. How was it that Paul could write with such feeling to Timothy, "from a child thou hast known the holy scriptures that are able to make thee wise unto salvation?" (2nd Tim. 3: 15) Two godly women, his mother and his grandmother, had taught Timothy to read. It would appear they may even have used the sacred text as his manual. Be that as it may, in one way or another, they instilled into his mind at an early age the scriptures of truth. This is the great thing for Christian parents to do. The Spirit of God can then work upon the precious seed, sown over many years and watered by earnest prayer.

But all this requires time and patience. Parents, and especially Christian mothers, neglect this to the lasting impoverishment of their children. Even if it means for a time foregoing some of the luxuries which so many falsely deem necessities, Christian mothers should remember for their children as well as for themselves how the Saviour said "Seek first the kingdom of God and His righteousness and all these things will be added unto you." (Matt. 6: 33)

THE NEW GENERATION

Noah and his wife enjoyed the blessing of household salvation. Their children heard the word of God. It came to them in the form of an invitation, "Come...into the ark." (Gen. 7: 1) Come is the characteristic word of the gospel. Jesus said, "Come unto me and him that cometh unto me I will in no wise cast out." (John 6: 37) Christian parents desire above all else that their children will be gathered into the larger family of God through faith in our Lord Jesus Christ. Journeying with two angels on their way to the destruction of Sodom, the Lord Himself, in one of His mysterious appearings in Old Testament times, turned aside and received the hospitality of Abraham and Sarah. Afterwards He said, "shall I hide from Abraham the thing that I do; for I know that he will command his children and his house-hold after him, and they shall keep the way of the Lord?"

(Gen. 18: 17-19) Christian parents will also covet for their children, that they too will learn to walk in the ways of the Lord. To this end they will recognise the value and power of a good example, for parents must themselves walk so that the children have objectively set before them a pattern of how they too should walk and please God.

An oft quoted verse from the Psalms says "from everlasting to everlasting thou art God."(Psa. 90: 2) The underlying thought seems to be, not just that God is in perpetuity, but that He is changeless throughout all generations. Ours is a changeful lot; but He is the unchanging one. With us generation succeeds generation, with all the mutations that mark the human story: but God is the same in every generation of His people. "Tell it to the generation following" was the advice given to those who went about Zion. (Psa. 48). We too have a responsibility to pass on to those who come after us, what we have known of the everlasting God.

Israel's honoured law-giver committed the oracles of God to his people with this charge, "teach them diligently unto your children." (Deut. 6: 7) Shall we do less who are privileged to live on the resurrection side of Calvary's cross. Children growing up in Christian homes should have some awareness of how John Bunyan proved God in Bedford gaol, and how William Carey was led to carry the gospel to the vast sub-continent of India, Hudson Taylor to China and C.T. Studd to Africa. Above all, such children should be instructed in the holy scriptures, that are able to make them wise unto salvation.

We cannot, of course, make Christians of our children; only the operation of the Spirit of God can accomplish that; but we can bring them up in the nuture and admonition of the Lord. It is a serious reproach upon Christian parents, when the children grow up with scarcely any knowledge of the things of God. If the good seed has not been faithfully and liberally sown in the young hearts and minds how can we claim we are looking to God to give the needed increase and to bring our children to spiritual life. These two vital exercises, bringing the children up for the Lord and counting upon the Lord for the children, constitute the basic duty of Christian parents, and that from the very earliest days of parenthood

THE CHURCH'S ROLE

Finally, besides a father's influence and a mother's influence there is the influence of the Christian Church. The local fellowship of Christians is a divine institution from which the Christian home should take its character. The Church exists to to be a vessel of divine testimony in its locality. The Christian home should reflect that testimony as a witness to all the other homes in the immediate vicinity. Sometimes the peace of a Church is disturbed and it must be conceded that the trouble is often occasioned by such a trifle that the disturbance is a reproach to any people. But Christian parents should be wise enough on such occasions to discern a working of the enemy, for there is on the part of the gates of hell an incessant warfare being fought against the Church. Moreover at such times parents need to remind themselves that the same enemy has designs upon their home and upon their children for "your adversary the devil, as a roaring lion, goes about seeking whom he may devour." (1st Pet. 5: 8)

It is important for the Christian home that it should be knitted closely into the fellowship of that local church where the parents have been led by God to find their spiritual home. This gives opportunity for all to fulfil the law of Christ, to bear one another's burdens and to be helpers one of another.

Here something needs to be said about the changing patterns in many churches. Traditional evangelical churches maintain that one of the Sunday services should be a definite evangelistic occasion at which the presence of unconverted people would be especially sought. The gospel of salvation would be clearly preached and sinners would be made aware of their need, warned of their danger and urged to seek the Lord and call upon His name in repentance and faith. In many churches however, this is no longer the case. A somewhat general ministry has taken the place of a forthright presentation of the specific and essentially saving truth of the gospel. The excuses heard are many, the principle one being that there are nowadays so few unconverted people attending.But preachers should bear in mind that as a fairly general rule at least six categories of people will be present:

1. Persons not yet converted.
2. Persons who think themselves converted but are not.
3. Persons who are not sure of their position.
4. Persons who may be in the valley of decision.
5. Young people approaching a water-shed in their lives.
6. Children who should be exposed to regular gospel preaching.

We must not underestimate the latter category. Christian parents desiring to see their offspring come to Christ should bring them regularly under the sound of faithful gospel preaching, and they should pray that God will make His Word effectual in their conversion. The word of God is living seed and should be sown in the hearts of our children while they are still of tender years. There is then in their hearts that which the Spirit of God can work upon and in His own time bring to fruition. In seeking the conversion of our children we must of course avoid bringing pressure to bear upon them to make a decision for which they may not be ready. To do so may well be counter-productive and could do untold harm. But we must be faithful in sowing the seed and in due season we shall reap if we faint not.

Church members also have a great responsibility for the children in their midst. Hannah could look upon Samuel in the temple and say "for this child I prayed." (1st Sam. 1: 27) We should take upon our hearts other children besides our own, that in time to come we might be able to look over the congregation and identify one here and another there and say for him or her I prayed.

It would not have been appropriate to conclude a study,

however brief, of the brides of Genesis without some reference to the importance of the Christian home. The theme could be enlarged upon with much profit since the importance of the subject is absolute. Our guide must be, not the latest fashion of this passing world, but that word which is forever settled in heaven. To set aside the Creator's instruction is a very heavy responsibility for anyone to assume, and inevitably a price will have to be paid. Happiness certainly does not lie in that direction. On the contrary Jesus said, "if you know these things happy are you if you do them." (John 13: 17)The only course for us as followers of Christ is to let the word of Christ dwell in us richly. It will prove a lamp to our feet and a light to our path and against a background of shattered relationships and broken homes ours will be the path that shines more and more unto the perfect day.

•••

We hope you enjoy this book.
Please return or renew it by the due date.

FREDDY
THE SUPER STAR

by NEILL CAMERON

David Fickling Books

With Special Thanks to Anthony Hinton and Katie Bennett

Freddy The Superstar
is a
DAVID FICKLING BOOK

First published in Great Britain in 2022 by
David Fickling Books,
31 Beaumont Street,
Oxford, OX1 2NP

Text and illustrations © Neill Cameron, 2022

978-1-78845-253-3

 WHO?

1 3 5 7 9 10 8 6 4 2

The right of Neill Cameron to be identified as the author and illustrator
of this work has been asserted in accordance with the
Copyright, Designs and Patents Act 1988.

All rights reserved. No part of this publication may be reproduced,
stored in a retrieval system, or transmitted in any form or by any means,
electronic, mechanical, photocopying, recording or otherwise,
without the prior permission of the publishers.

Papers used by David Fickling Books are from well-managed
forests and other responsible sources.

GOOD

MIX
Paper from
responsible sources
FSC
www.fsc.org   FSC® C018072

DAVID FICKLING BOOKS Reg. No. 8340307

A CIP catalogue record for this book is
available from the British Library.

Printed and bound in Great Britain by Clays, Ltd, Elcograf SpA.